PIANO/VOCAL/CHORDS

100 YEARS OF POPULAR MUSIC

30s - Volume 1

Series Editor:
Carol Cuellar

Editorial and Production:
Artemis Music Limited

Design and Production:
JPCreativeGroup.com

Published 2003

International Music Publications Limited
Griffin House 161 Hammersmith Road London W6 8BS England

International MUSIC Publications

CONTENTS

30s

For most of the world the 1930s really began on October 29, 1929. It was on that "Black Tuesday" that the American stock market crashed, setting off the Great Depression that would plague almost every nation on earth for close to an entire decade.

During the darkest days of this international calamity, over 30 million people in the industrialised world were unemployed. By 1932, the total value of world trade had fallen to less than half of its pre-crash levels. In the UK, sterling lost 28 per cent of its value after the Bank of England left the gold standard in 1931. A year later, 22 per cent of adult male workers in Britain were without a job.

As dreadful as they appear, these numbers tell only part of the story of the Great Depression. Throughout Europe and America, the economic catastrophe drove millions to despair, tearing apart families and undermining faith in the basic principles of democracy.

The deepening crisis provided fertile ground for Fascists like Hitler and Mussolini to spread their malignant philosophy by both propaganda and force. In 1931, militaristic Japan invaded Manchuria. When Nazi Germany withdrew from the League of Nations two years later, and Fascist Italy conquered

Ethiopia in 1935, the shadows cast by the Great Depression grew even darker as war clouds gathered over Europe and Asia.

Music For Troubled Times

As it has so often done throughout history, music provided the people of the '30s with a welcome refuge from a turbulent and troubled world. In happy defiance of the decade's economic and political woes, many of its most popular songs took a decidedly optimistic view of life, love, and human nature.

Even today, well into a new century, listening to '30s hits like "On The Sunny Side Of The Street", "I've Got The World On A String", or "I've Got Rhythm" seems to bring an extra dash of élan to our spirit and buoyancy to our step. One can readily envision crowds at West End halls happily dancing the night away to the merry strains of these songs. In so doing, these young men and women were (deliberately or not) sending an unmistakable message to the invisible economic forces, and the all-too-known totalitarian despots of their day – we will not allow you to dampen our spirit!

Dorothy Fields (one of the earliest successful female songwriters) and Jimmy McHugh wrote "On The Sunny Side Of The Street" in 1930 for the stage production *International Revue*, starring British actress and entertainer Gertrude Lawrence. Debuting as it did at the very onset of the Great Depression, the song was a very conscious attempt to elevate spirits following the stock market crash.

"On The Sunny Side Of The Street" succeeded quite well in achieving this goal. The song's popularity far outlasted the Great Depression. In years to come, it would be recorded by a variety of superstars ranging from Louis Armstrong to Willie Nelson.

Like the song itself, performer Gertrude Lawrence epitomised the unfailing optimism and spirit that helped the people of the '30s fight back against economic adversity. Born to a theatrical family around the turn of the century in London, Lawrence became a stage star while still in her early teens. Her fame already well established when the '30s dawned, she continued to project an image of style and grace during the lean years with her elegant dress and sophisticated tastes.

Music Gives Voice To Hopes And Nostalgia

Still, try as they might to face adversity with a brave – and even elegant – face, the people of the '30s must have yearned on occasion for an easier, simpler, and certainly less ominous bygone era. This longing is evident in many of the popular songs of the decade. Among the most memorable tunes in this category is the heartfelt "Over The Rainbow" from the film *The Wizard of Oz*.

The Harold Arlen and E.Y. "Yip" Harburg tune was made famous throughout the world by Judy Garland, who played Dorothy in the hit film. Seldom have a performer and song been so well suited to one another as the 16-year-old Garland and "Over The Rainbow". As light and ethereal as a rainbow itself, her rendition of this song offered an almost mystical sense of transformation to weary Depression-era audiences.

Like Dorothy, who had been whisked up form her Kansas home by a tornado and transported to the Land of Oz, the majority of people in the '30s had seen their lives blown off course by the winds of economic and political upheaval. Somehow, listening to Garland's angelic voice sing "Over The Rainbow", one couldn't help but share Dorothy's hope for a better tomorrow.

Sweet romantic songs also offered a chance to escape from the gritty day-to-day struggles of the Great Depression. In 1936, when economic burdens seemed all the heavier as a result of the looming spectre of war in Europe, the soft and haunting Jerome Kern and Dorothy Fields song "The Way You Look Tonight" became a runaway hit.

This achingly beautiful song was released only three years before Hitler's invasion of Poland marked the start of World War II. Listen to it closely. Beneath the gentle melody and sweet lyrics, one can feel the growing sense of apprehension over a looming separation.

"Someday, when I'm awfully low,
When the world is cold,
I will feel a glow just thinking of you...
And the way you look tonight."

In this song, a young lover is trying to freeze a special moment, to capture an image forever and lock it away in the deepest recesses of memory, so that it may be brought out on some cold and distant day to warm the heart and comfort the soul. It is a romantic notion shared by lovers in every generation, but how real it became at the end of the '30s when the millions of couples separated by war were joined only by their shared memory of such moments.

Jerome Kern, who wrote the music for "The Way You Look Tonight", was a New Yorker who went to London at 19 and sharpened his musical skills working on West End stage productions. Kern and Fields wrote the song for the film *Swing Time*, starring Fred

Astaire and Ginger Rogers. Performed by Astaire, the song won an Academy Award.

Relaxed, smooth and elegant, Astaire, playing the role of gambler Lucky Garnett, was perfectly suited to sing "The Way You Look Tonight". His precarious occupation lent an added dimension to the current of uncertainty running beneath the song's surface.

A Decade Of Musical Firsts

The '30s were also a time of "firsts" for music. It was during this decade that singers (or crooners as they were called) first became comfortable with microphones. It was also the decade when the film soundtrack and pre-recorded music truly came into their own. And it was the time when the swing band first appeared.

Swing orchestras gave much of the world its first exposure to a new generation of African-American jazz artists. A leading member of this group was the tenor saxophonist Coleman Hawkins. A gifted improviser who is widely regarded as the pioneer of the

tenor saxophone, Hawkins first achieved notoriety in the US as a member of the Fletcher Henderson Orchestra, a group that also included Louis Armstrong.

In 1934, Hawkins moved to Europe, joining Jack Hylton's Orchestra in the UK. He remained in Europe for five years, enthralling audiences with his dynamic style, as evident in his signature tune "Body And Soul".

From the sweet sentimentality of "Over The Rainbow," to the hot tenor of Coleman Hawkins, the '30s brought us unforgettable music in a variety of styles. So enjoy our sampler of '30s sounds. It offers irrefutable proof that even the toughest of times can't stifle the musical voice within us.

Ten Things That First Appeared In The '30s

1. **The jet engine, developed by British pilot and engineer Frank Whittle.**

2. **Air defence radar stations, first installed in England (1938).**

3. **Superman character, introduced in comics.**

4. **The planet Pluto, discovered in 1930.**

5. **Toyota automobiles.**

6. **Paperback books.**

7. **The helicopter.**

8. **The electric razor.**

9. **FM radio.**

10. **Pre-packaged sliced bread.**

ALL I DO IS DREAM OF YOU

Words by ARTHUR FREED
Music by NACIO HERB BROWN

Out of a clear blue sky, in - to my heart you came,
When ev - ery day be - gins, when ev - ery day is done,

not for a day, but here to stay, I'll al - ways feel the same.
here in my heart, ne - ver to part, You'll al - ways be the one.

ABOUT A QUARTER TO NINE

Words by AL DUBIN
Music by HARRY WARREN

ALL OF ME

Words and Music by SEYMOUR SIMONS and GERALD MARKS

ALL THE THINGS YOU ARE

Words by OSCAR HAMMERSTEIN II
Music by JEROME KERN

ANYTHING GOES

Words and Music by COLE PORTER

BEYOND THE BLUE HORIZON

Words by LEO ROBIN
Music by RICHARD A WHITING and W FRANKE HARLING

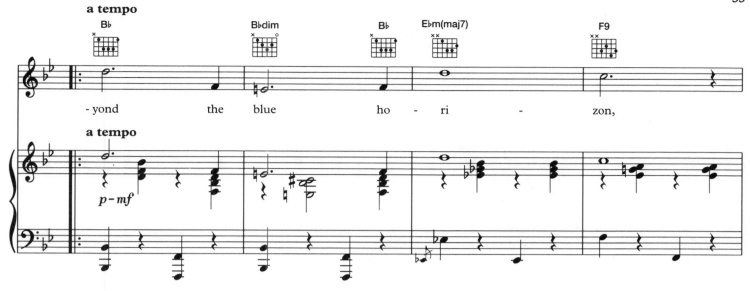

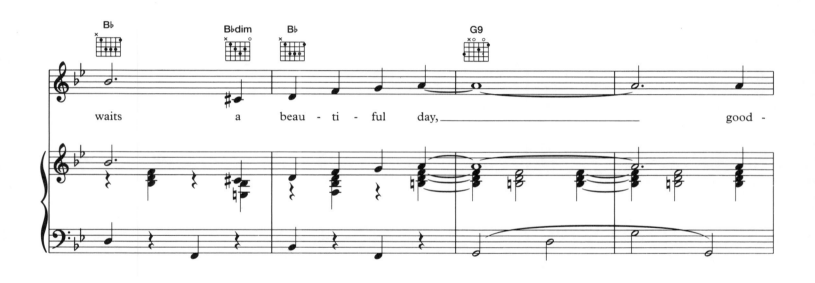

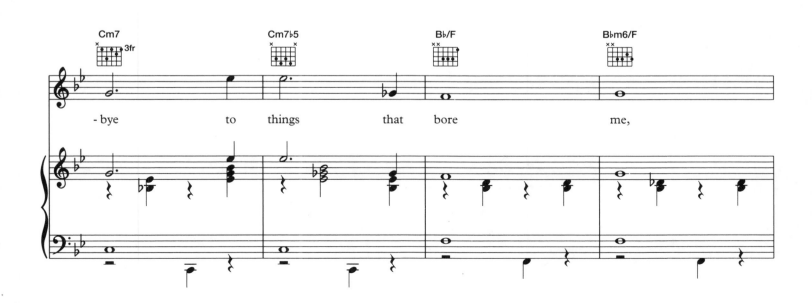

-yond the blue ho - ri - zon lies a

ris - ing sun. _____ Be -

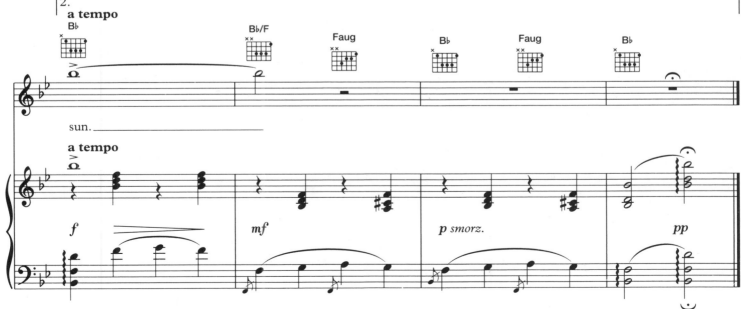

sun. _____

BLUE MOON

Words by LORENZ HART
Music by RICHARD RODGERS

Once up-on a time, be my
Once up-on a time, my

BODY AND SOUL

Words by ROBERT SOUR, EDWARD HEYMAN
and FRANK EYTON
Music by JOHNNY GREEN

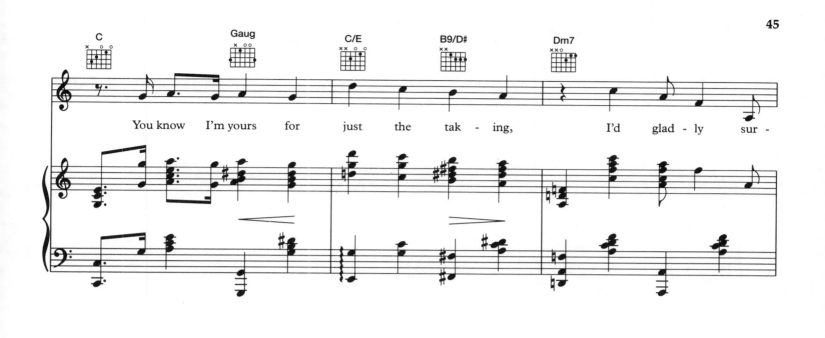

You know I'm yours for just the tak - ing, I'd glad - ly sur -

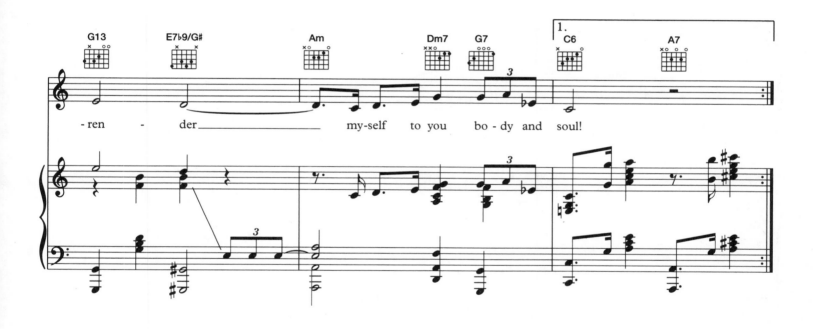

- ren - der _____ my-self to you bo - dy and soul!

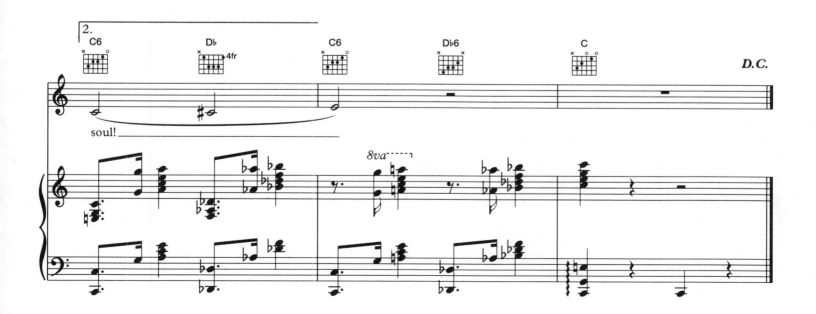

soul! _____

D.C.

BYE BYE BLUES

Words and Music by FRED HAMM, DAVE BENNETT,
BERT LOWN and CHAUNCEY GRAY

DANCING WITH TEARS IN MY EYES

Words by AL DUBIN
Music by JOE BURKE

DEEP PURPLE

Words by MITCHELL PARISH
Music by PETER DE ROSE

DINNER FOR ONE PLEASE JAMES

Words and Music by MICHAEL CARR

James has been but-ler to Mis-ter B___ for fif-ty years, come Au-gust three, and he

still re-mem-bers the night of his mas-ter's tra-ge-dy.___

Mas-ter's best friend was a Mis-ter J,___ James did-n't like him

seems my best friend told her of an - oth - er, I had no chance to de - ny.

You know there has ne - ver been an - oth - er. Some day she'll find out the lie,

may - be she's not to blame. Leave me with si - lent hours, __ no,

don't move her fav - ourite flo - wers, din - ner for one please, James.' James.'

DANCING IN THE DARK

Words by HOWARD DIETZ
Music by ARTHUR SCHWARTZ

FOR ALL WE KNOW

Words by SAM LEWIS
Music by J FRED COOTS

EMBRACEABLE YOU

Music and Lyrics by GEORGE GERSHWIN and IRA GERSHWIN

He: Doz-ens of girls would storm up,
She: I went a-bout re-cit - ing,

I had to lock my door.
'Here's one who ne - ver fall!'

Some-how I could - n't warm_ up to
But I'm a-fraid the writ - ing is

one be - fore.
on the wall.

What was it that con-trolled_ me?
My nose I used to turn_ up,

A FOGGY DAY

Music and Lyrics by GEORGE GERSHWIN and IRA GERSHWIN

I was a stran-ger in the ci-ty,_____ out of town were the peo-ple I knew.

I had that feel-ing of self pi-ty,_____ what to do? What to do? What to do? The

FOR YOU

Words by AL DUBIN
Music by JOE BURKE

GET HAPPY

Words and Music by HAROLD ARLEN and TED KOEHLER

THE GLORY OF LOVE

Words and Music by BILLY HILL

You've got to give a lit-tle, take a lit-tle, and let your poor heart break a lit-tle, that's the sto-ry of, that's the glo-ry of love. You've got to

GOODY GOODY

Words and Music by JOHNNY MERCER and MATT MALNECK

Moderately bright and swingy

You told me there was-n't a les - son in lov-in' that you had-n't learned. Oh

yeah? _____ Oh yeah? _____ You

HOMETOWN

Words by MICHAEL CARR
Music by JIMMY KENNEDY

I APOLOGISE

Words and Music by AL HOFFMAN,
AL GOODHART and ED G NELSON

I DON'T KNOW WHY (I JUST DO!)

Words by ROY TURK
Music by FRED E AHLERT

I GOT RHYTHM

Music and Lyrics by GEORGE GERSHWIN and IRA GERSHWIN

I GUESS I'LL HAVE TO CHANGE MY PLAN

Words by HOWARD DIETZ
Music by ARTHUR SCHWARTZ

I WANNA BE LOVED BY YOU

Words by BERT KALMAR
Music by HERBERT STOTHART and HARRY RUBY

I ONLY HAVE EYES FOR YOU

Words by AL DUBIN
Music by HARRY WARREN

Are the stars out to-night? ___ I don't know if it's clou-dy or bright, ___ 'cause I on-ly have eyes ___ for you, ___ dear. ___ The moon may be high, ___ but I

I WON'T DANCE

Words by OSCAR HAMMERSTEIN II, OTTO HARBACH,
DOROTHY FIELDS and JIMMY McHUGH
Music by JEROME KERN

I'LL STRING ALONG WITH YOU

Words by AL DUBIN
Music by HARRY WARREN

All my life I wait-ed for an an - gel, but no an-gel ev - er came a - long.

Then one hap-py af - ter-noon I met you, and my heart be-gan to sing a song.

Some-how, I mis-took you for an an - gel, but now I'm glad that I was wrong.

You may not be an an - gel, 'cause an - gels are so

few,

but un - til the day that one comes a - long,

I'll string a - long with you.

I'm look - ing for an

I'M CONFESSIN'

Words by AL NEIBURG
Music by DOC DAUGHERTY and ELLIS REYNOLDS

I'm con-fess-in' that I need you, hon-est I do, need you ev-ery mo-ment!

In your eyes I read such strange things, but your lips de-ny they're true.

Will your ans-wer real-ly change things, mak-ing me blue? _____

I'm a-fraid some-day you'll leave me, say-ing, 'Can't we still be friends?'

I'M IN THE MOOD FOR LOVE

Words by DOROTHY FIELDS
Music by JIMMY McHUGH

I'M SHOOTING HIGH

Words by TED KOEHLER
Additional Words by CHARLES WILMOTT
Music by JIMMY McHUGH

Ev - ery morn - ing when I raise my blind to
Ev - ery night I won - der when we part, and

I'VE GOT THE WORLD ON A STRING

Words and Music by TED KOEHLER and HAROLD ARLEN

I'VE TOLD EV'RY LITTLE STAR

Words by OSCAR HAMMERSTEIN II
Music by JEROME KERN

IN A SHANTY IN OLD SHANTY TOWN

Words by JOE YOUNG
Music by LITTLE JACK LITTLE and JOHN SIRAS

poco rit.

best,   means   more   than   the   world   to   me. _____   It's
true,   to   me   it   is   pa - ra - dise. _____

a tempo

on - ly   a   shan - ty   in   old   Shan - ty   Town, _____   the

roof   is   so   slan - ty,   it   touch - es   the   ground,   but   my   tum - bled   down

shack,   by   an   old   rail - road   track,   like   a   mil - lion - aire's   man - sion,   is

I'VE GOT YOU UNDER MY SKIN

Words and Music by COLE PORTER

warn - ing voice that comes in the night, and re - peats and re - peats in my

subito p

ear, _____ 'Don't you know, lit - tle fool, _____ you ne - ver can

molto cresc.   *f molto espressivo*

win? _____ Use your men - ta - li - ty,_____

_ wake up to re - al - i - ty.'_____ But each

mf

time I do, just the thought of you makes me stop be-fore I be - gin, 'cause I've

got you_____ un-der my skin._____ I've

I've

ISLE OF CAPRI

Words by JIMMY KENNEDY
Music by WILHELM GROSZ

IT'S ONLY A PAPER MOON

Words by BILLY ROSE and E Y HARBURG
Music by HAROLD ARLEN

IT'S THE TALK OF THE TOWN

Words by MARTY SYMES and AL NEIBURG
Music by JERRY LEVINSON

We were more than lov - ers, we were more than sweet - hearts, it's so hard to un - der -

JUST ONE MORE CHANCE

Words by SAM COSLOW
Music by ARTHUR JOHNSTON

We spend our lives in grop-ing for hap-pi-ness,____
I had one chance, but I did-n't go for it,____

I found it once, and tossed it a - side.____
I threw a - way, the joy that I had.____

KEEP YOUNG AND BEAUTIFUL

Words by AL DUBIN
Music by HARRY WARREN

IT'S A SIN TO TELL A LIE

Words and Music by BILLY MAYHEW

You
The

know it's a sin to tell a lie, still you keep
love that I give you dear will live, not for a

say - ing, 'I love you!' _____ It may be true,
day, but for - ev - er. _____ So don't pre - tend,

THE LADY IS A TRAMP

Words by LORENZ HART
Music by RICHARD RODGERS

LET'S FALL IN LOVE

Words by TED KOEHLER
Additional Words by CHARLES WILMOTT
Music by HAROLD ARLEN

I have a feel - ing, it's a feel - ing I'm con - ceal - ing, I don't know why.
Love fails you ne - ver, his en - deav - our is for - ev - er fate to de - fy,

It's just a men - tal, in - ci - den - tal, sen - ti - men - tal a - li - bi, but
comes to you steal - ing with his feel - ing, and ap - peal - ing lul - la - by. He

LET BY-GONES BE BY-GONES

Words and Music by J G GILBERT

Some-times a word that is spo-ken,_____ makes some-one
This world was once in con-fu-sion,_____ through self-ish

lone-ly and blue,_____ leav-ing a heart that is
things that were done,_____ this is my on-ly con-

LIFE IS JUST A BOWL OF CHERRIES

Words and Music by LEW BROWN and RAY HENDERSON

LOVE IS JUST AROUND THE CORNER

Words and Music by LEO ROBIN and LEWIS E GENSLER

LOVE LETTERS IN THE SAND

Words by NICK KENNY and CHARLES KENNY
Music by J FRED COOTS

The sun-beams kissed the sands, my fate was in your hands,
While pre-cious tear-drops fall, your mem-ory I re-call,

the day I met you dear. ____
and days that used to be. ____

197

LOVELY LADY

Words by TED KOEHLER
Music by JIMMY McHUGH

Reach - ing for moon - beams, oh heart of mine,
There's a new glo - ry dawn - ing for me,

MEMORIES OF YOU

Words by ANDY RAZAF
Music by EUBIE BLAKE

MUSIC, MAESTRO, PLEASE!

Words by HERBERT MAGIDSON
Music by ALLIE WRUBEL

ON THE SUNNY SIDE OF THE STREET

Words by DOROTHY FIELDS
Music by JIMMY McHUGH

MOONLIGHT SERENADE

Words by MITCHELL PARISH
Music by GLENN MILLER

ONCE IN A WHILE

Words by BUD GREEN
Music by MICHAEL EDWARDS

OVER THE RAINBOW

Words by E Y HARBURG
Music by HAROLD ARLEN

PICK YOURSELF UP

Words by DOROTHY FIELDS
Music by JEROME KERN

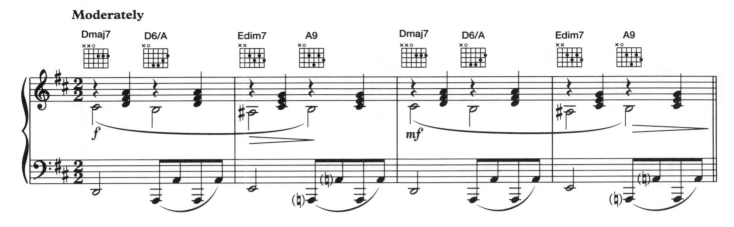

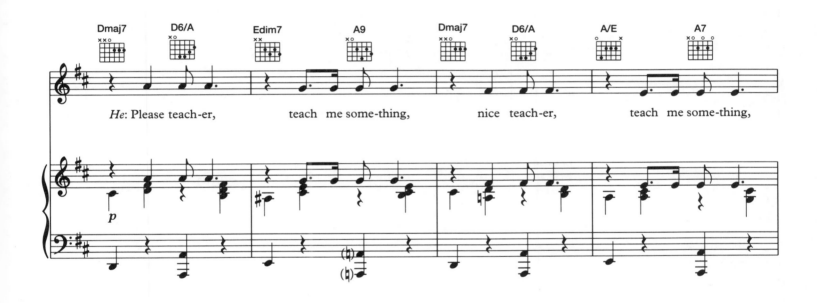

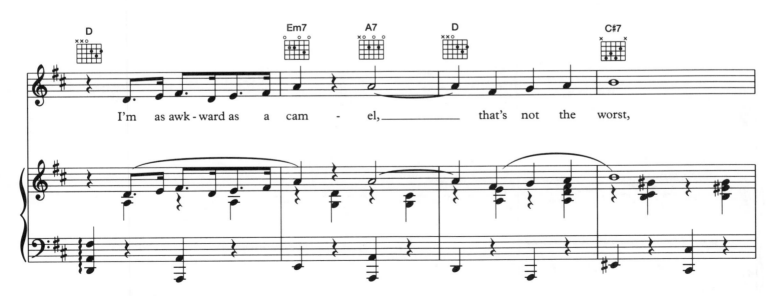

PARADISE

Words and Music by NACIO HERB BROWN and GORDON CLIFFORD

Keith Prowse Music Pub Co Ltd, London WC2H 0EA

PLEASE DON'T TALK ABOUT ME WHEN I'M GONE

Words by SIDNEY CLARE
Music by SAM STEPT

RED SAILS IN THE SUNSET

Words by JIMMY KENNEDY
Music by HUGH WILLIAMS

'Twas down where fish-er-folk ga-ther, I wan-dered far from the throng, I
Red sails, the night breeze is blow-ing, and clouds are hid-ing the moon, I a-

heard a fish-er-girl sing-ing, and this re-frain was her song.
-bove no bright stars are glow-ing, it means the storm's com-ing soon.

SMOKE GETS IN YOUR EYES

Words by OTTO HARBACH
Music by JEROME KERN

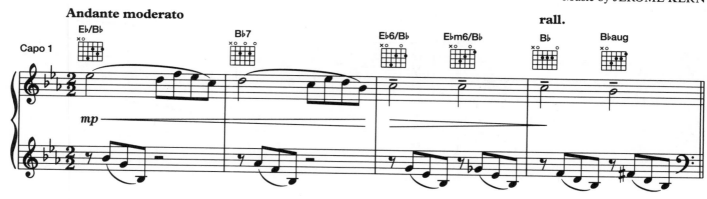

They asked me how I knew, my true love was true.

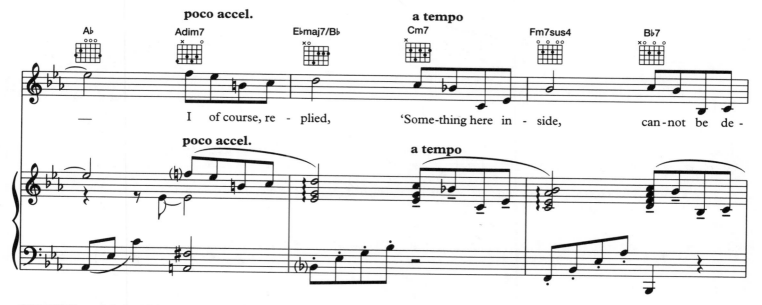

I of course, re-plied, 'Some-thing here in - side, can-not be de-

PolyGram Music Publishing Ltd, London W4 2NL

SAN FRANCISCO

Words by GUS KAHN
Music by BRONISLAW KAPER and WALTER JURMANN

It on-ly takes a ti-ny cor-ner of____

SEPTEMBER IN THE RAIN

Words by AL DUBIN
Music by HARRY WARREN

My day dreams lie bur-ied in au-tumn leaves, they're cov-ered with au-tumn
Now warm spring is fill-ing my life with dreams, that I thought all past and

rain, the time is sweet Sep - tem - ber,
gone, but still there ev - er lin - gers

Fm7♭5
B♭7
E♭
B♭7♯5
-tem - ber, in the rain. The
E♭
Gm
Cm
Gm
Fm
sun went out just like a dy - ing em - ber, that Sep -
Fm7♭5
B♭7
E♭
-tem - ber, in the rain. To
B♭m7
E♭7
B♭m7
E♭7
A♭
ev - ery word of love I heard you whis - per, the
3

SEPTEMBER SONG

Words by MAXWELL ANDERSON
Music by KURT WEILL

SOUTH OF THE BORDER

Words and Music by JIMMY KENNEDY and MICHAEL CARR

258

WHO'S TAKING YOU HOME TONIGHT

Words and Music by TOMMIE CONNOR and MANNING SHERWIN

STAR DUST

Words by MITCHELL PARISH
Music by HOAGY CARMICHAEL

STAY AS SWEET AS YOU ARE

Words and Music by MACK GORDON and HARRY REVEL

TEMPTATION

Words by ARTHUR FREED
Music by NACIO HERB BROWN

THANKS FOR THE MEMORY

Words and Music by LEO ROBIN and RALPH RAINGER

THERE'S A SMALL HOTEL

Words by LORENZ HART
Music by RICHARD RODGERS

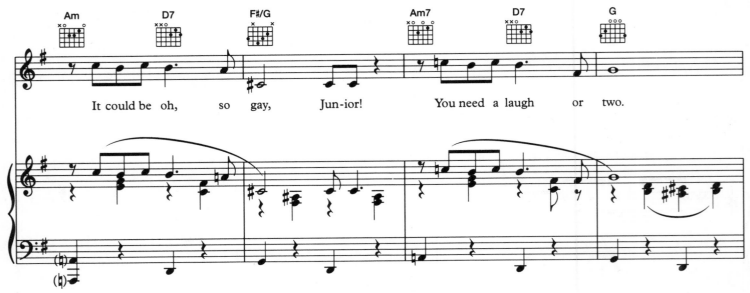

THREE LITTLE WORDS

Words by BERT KALMAR
Music by HARRY RUBY

WALKIN' MY BABY BACK HOME

Words and Music by ROY TURK and FRED E AHLERT

Lyrics:

I've an a-gree-ab-le ba - by likes ev-ery-thing_ that I do,_
Gee, but it's great_ when my ba - by tells me she'll see_ me that night,_

dan-ces most ev - ery night, mov-ies are her_ de-light,
I look up roads_ to go that no one else_ would know

290

THE WAY YOU LOOK TONIGHT

Words by DOROTHY FIELDS
Music by JEROME KERN

WHAT A DIFFERENCE A DAY MADE

Spanish Words and Music by MARIA GREVER
English Words by STANLEY ADAMS

WHEN I TAKE MY SUGAR TO TEA

Words and Music by SAMMY FAIN, IRVING KAHAL
and PIERRE NORMAN

ne - ver take her where the gang goes,___ when I take my su - gar to

tea._____ I'm a row - dy dow - dy that's me,_____ she's a high hat ba - by, that's

she,_____ so I ne - ver take her where the gang goes,___ when I

take my su - gar to tea. Ev - ery Sun - day af - ter - noon_

WHERE OR WHEN

Words by LORENZ HART
Music by RICHARD RODGERS

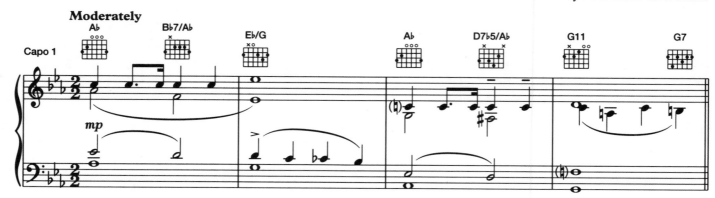

305

YOU CAME ALONG (FROM OUT OF NOWHERE)

Words by EDWARD HEYMAN
Music by JOHNNY GREEN

YOU MUST HAVE BEEN A BEAUTIFUL BABY

Words by JOHNNY MERCER
Music by HARRY WARREN

YOU'RE MY EVERYTHING

Words by MORT DIXON and JOE YOUNG
Music by HARRY WARREN

YOUNG AND HEALTHY

Words by AL DUBIN
Music by HARRY WARREN

100 YEARS OF POPULAR MUSIC

International
MUSIC
Publications

IMP's Exciting New Series!

100 YEARS OF POPULAR MUSIC

Vol. 1 - 9817A

9816A

Vol. 1 - 9819A

Vol. 1 - 9821A

Vol. 1 - 9823A

Vol. 2 - 9818A

Vol. 2 - 9820A

Vol. 2 - 9822A

Vol. 2 - 9824A

IMP
International
MUSIC
Publications

IMP's Exciting New Series!

100 YEARS OF POPULAR MUSIC

Vol. 1 - 9825A

Vol. 1 - 9827A

Vol. 1 - 9829A

Vol. 1 - 9831A

Vol. 2 - 9826A

Vol. 2 - 9828A

Vol. 2 - 9830A

Vol. 2 - 9832A

Vol. 2 - 9833A

International
MUSIC
Publications

IMP's Exciting New Series!